Reac

The Place of the Peo

Duncan Mackay is a former winner of the Henry Ford European Conservation Award for Heritage and former editor of the Twyford and Ruscombe Local History Society magazine.

He has worked as Director of the South East region of the Countryside Agency; Environmental Manager for Berkshire County Council; and Deputy Secretary of the Commons, Open Spaces and Footpaths Preservation Society.

He has written five books and contributed to others including *England in Particular* and *Bastions of Berkshire*.

First published in the UK in 2016 by Two Rivers Press
7 Denmark Road, Reading RG1 5PA
www.tworiverspress.com

ISBN 978-1-909747-23-4

1 2 3 4 5 6 7 8 9

Two Rivers Press is represented in the UK by Inpress Ltd
and distributed by NBN International.

Cover design by Nadja Guggi with an illustration by Peter Hay
Text design by Nadja Guggi and typeset in Parisine

Printed and bound in Great Britain by Imprint Digital, Exeter

To my 'little' brother Ian Mackay

Acknowledgements

I offer my huge thanks to Robert Macfarlane for providing such an inspiring foreword. Rob and I share a passion for landscapes and travel writing and he has won literary awards for *Mountains of the Mind*, *The Wild Places*, *The Old Ways* and *Landmarks*. Rob and I also share an interest in the creation of 'new commons' as a means to provide new green spaces close to where people live. Watch that space.

Thanks to the Two Rivers Press team: Sally Mortimore, who commissioned the book, Barbara Morris and Adam Sowan, who subtly massaged it into shape. Nadja Guggi translated my revolutionary poster ideas into the covers and sneaked the late Pete Hay's eclectic catalogue of artworks around my unyielding format. Thanks to previous authors of books on Reading; in particular I have borrowed from Daphne Phillips, John Paul Nash and Stuart Hylton. The map of the three Parishes of Reading is from Geoff Sawers' *Broad Street Chapel* and I'm grateful for his permission to include it. Some odd nuggets were mined from the adits of the ever-helpful Mr Wiki. Bless Henry Marchant for being ready to serve.

My wife Viv has stoically put up with my dark winter of domestic dislocation; researching, writing and being in striking distance of the Muse, with her typical good humour and forbearance.

Finally, I'd like to thank the United Nations of carers at the Royal Berkshire Hospital who worked through the frantic Christmas of 2015 when I was admitted with acute pneumonia. I hope that my thanks to Portuguese nurse Margarita Teixeira will serve for all.

Foreword

'Place is always moving, like a sleeping cat', observed the Japanese artist Toshiya Tsunoda beautifully in 2011. But the 'movements' of place are mostly hard for the human eye to perceive, for they occur over timescales (aeons, epochs, eras, centuries) that exceed the usual units of our apprehension (minutes, days, months, years). Here, Duncan Mackay makes vividly visible the movements of the sleeping cat of Reading, the Red One. His deep-time journey tours us from the coccolith snow-storms of the Cretaceous to the town's hopeful possible futures, by way of Bronze Age smelters, the English Civil War and the opening in 1968 of the Didcot Power Station, the 'Cathedral of the Vale', the exhaust gases of which 'formed new cloudscapes visible for fifty miles in all directions'. His knowledge is remarkable, and his voice distinctive in its wit and passion. What emerges is a layered sense of how a landscape's deep structures bear shapingly upon its surface textures – and how vital a sense of place is to our dreams, our visions, and the quiet practices of everyday life.

Robert Macfarlane

Introduction

Reading has been variously described as 'very large and wealthy' (*Tour Through the Whole Island of Great Britain*, Daniel Defoe 1724) and 'fairly hideous' (*Rough Guide to England* 1996). These contrary opinions are mere snapchats in time, of a location that periodically thrusts cues at its visitors. What they underscore is the constancy of change in the fabric of the complex thing that we call 'place'.

The mission of this little book is to explore the many historic landscapes of Reading to uncover fragments of the reasons for it being here, its variety of configurations through time and some snippets from the life of its inhabitants to colour our cares or prejudices. There will never be a complete story of the interactions of past peoples and this geography but I hope that there will be a trail of sufficiently large biscuit crumbs for you to follow your way back through the past to speculate on its *genius loci*. I fear that we will not totally nail it but it might plant a seed that there is more to 'anywhere' than what 'anyone' can tell you. However, we will not limit our imagination but also speculate about the geological origins of the landform

of the Reading area and the unseen, tiniest, microscopic life forms that created some of the largest elements of the bigger picture that is Reading's face upon the Earth.

The *European Landscape Convention* boldly declares that 'all landscapes matter'. So we should be emboldened to beautify the places that matter to us *and* to enhance the prospects of securing a sufficiency of food, water and shelter for our health and happiness but without compromising the needs of others from whom we acquire these commodities. In former times these factors would combine very closely in a small landscape geography, but in times of Empire and in our globalised economy the extended landscape and services required to satisfy Reading's current wants stretch for thousands of miles. Reading was also subject to people from faraway places who came *here* as farmers, settlers, invaders, pilgrims, industrialisers or economic migrants. Reada, the person who possibly gave Reading its name, probably in the sixth century AD, migrated here with his people from the coastal landscape that is now shared between Germany and Denmark. He (the Red One) most likely arrived by boat with other invading kinfolk such as Sunna, Woca and Basa, bringing their culture and genes to the local Romano-Celtic peoples. We do not know if this was a happy engagement or a marriage of convenience, but it was significant.

So, from the genetic hotch-potch of the past to the kaleidoscope of potential futures we end with a sense of Reading's place as a future city, perhaps as one of the World's first National Park Cities, set in a graceful green hinterland.

The White Stuff

c. 145 – 65 million years ago

The Town of Biscuits is built on a solid base of white chalk, knobbly nodules of siliceous flint, a scattering of crunchy gravel and definitely, although infrequently, suffers a soggy bottom of Thames flood alluvium. Chalk is the stuff of old schools and blackboard lessons. Chalk is the source of one half of the expression 'like chalk and cheese'. However, unlike the contrary topographical violence of Scottish volcanic plugs, which created places like Edinburgh, it is a humble builder of broad-backed southern softy landscapes. It is easy to overlook chalk except where it is cut by the sea when, unprompted, it forms nationalistic White Cliffs or, where cut by human hands, forms

horses and even dragons on green hillsides. The chalk of Reading is somewhat shy but can be felt by walking from the river to the University or by a spot of weeding in the riverfront Hanging Gardens of Caversham, where a dash of dirty white can be glimpsed amidst the trees. For a little bit of unwanted drama, however, Reading's chalk can provide excitement, especially if your house is built over the top of an undisclosed chalk mine. This is Reading's secret. These unrecorded catacombs of an industrial underground whose excavators, like blind moles, wandered 'thither of themselves' picking at the white stuff. Then, a century or so later, add an enthusiastic cloudburst or two, and 'whoosh' your cosy sitting room might become an impromptu damp basement.

What exactly is this deceitful white stuff? Have you ever swum at night in a sparkling green bioluminescent sea? If you have, then you will know the startling impression that vast numbers of microscopic phosphorescent creatures can make on the human soul. We need to view chalk with similar reverence. Chalk is the cadaverous mass of centillions (10^{600}) of ancient coccolithophores. Surging swarms of these microscopic marine organisms unwittingly sacrificed themselves to regulate the carbon chemistry of the oceans *and* the atmosphere and bring balance to the world; they were the nano-fossil Zen masters of the Cretaceous period (145–65 million years ago). Millions of years later their Yoda-like relatives are still doing the same gig and their tiny, tiny bodies are falling like snow through the dark depths to form calcareous ooze that covers over one third of the oceanic floor. Add some time and bake at low heat to make the chalk cake of the future.

Orogenous Zones

c. 60 million years ago

Any winter's day, travellers can be seen at Reading Station adjusting their crampons and preparing to mount the first steps of their alpine skiing holidays at the doorway of the Heathrow RailAir link bus or shuffling mysterious ironing-board size, Gatwick-bound, padded bundles towards platform 4.

Dig beneath the modern concrete of the station concourse, scour through the underlying recent alluvium and glacial gravel until you hit that white wonder, the Cretaceous Chalk. There is a powerful link, a binding, between these expectant alpinists and Reading's bedrock but you don't need to leave the country to experience it. This is the Wonder of the Land of Knowledge rather than the Winter Wonderland of Glügg and Sausage. So, what's the big deal? Power beyond your wildest dreams... that's what, and evidence of it is right beneath your feet wherever you stand in Reading. You can't feel Switzerland in your kitchens or Italy in your bedrooms but the massive effect of the impact of the Alpine Orogeny that started *c.* 60 million years ago has created the basic landform of Reading that is visible in all directions. In this complex episode of crustal shuffling, bits of the Earth's surface, like clustered croutons floating on the top of thick soup, were propelled towards each other. The motive power for this movement was not the back of a giant soupspoon but unseen hot spots of upwelling mantle creating a push effect on the crusty bits. The repercussion of this outwards spreading was that Africa put the squeeze on Europe and Italy in particular responded by forming itself into a crushing wedge.

The immediate and most obvious result of this slow-speed shunt were the uplifted Alps, Apennines, Pyrenees, Atlas, Rif, Caucasus and Transylvanian mountain chains but the impact of the crushing pressure travelled much further. Indeed, the ripples reached Reading and the semi-plastic beds of chalk folded and warped like a loose hall carpet. Subsequent erosion by rivers and glacial impacts has exposed the rocky core of this crumpled orogenous zone and thereby provides Reading with the basic shape of its landscape today and an unlikely link to the Alps.

Reading Beds

c. 5 million years ago

Tens of millions of years after the deposition of the chalk and the start of the Alpine Orogeny, the most significant of Reading's economic geology events took place about 5 million years ago during the geological period called the Eocene. An unnamed river dropped sedimentary deposits of clays, sands and the gloriously named 'puddingstones' into an unnamed sea. These layered beds of soft rock and clays are now deemed to be part of the Lambeth Group, which sounds more like a gathering of left wing borough councillors rather than a serious sequence of rocky deposits. Amidst this was once the Reading Beds (not to be confused with a bedroom furniture showroom) but these have now suffered a name change to the infinitely clearer Reading Formation, which sounds like a synchro early learning project. Surely there really should be a local support group (Facebook page, Twitter account etc) for this unique geological configuration that has its type locality in and around Reading?

The Reading Formation clastics (think sticky) and the adjacent thick band of marine clay formerly known as the London Clay have played an important part in the making of the physical fabric of the town of Reading. In prehistoric times, when settled agriculture was established from the Neolithic onwards, the natural advantage provided by useful local clay for making storage and cooking pots was probably keenly sought. Workable clay, like plentiful wood, good water and local food supplies were essential place-making adjuncts to early peoples. Through the much later medieval period, clay was still important, particularly for wattle and daub house building and

cheap, crude pottery. In Tudor and Elizabethan times hand-made bricks from local clay built mansions for the wealthy like the Blounts at Mapledurham House, started in 1585 and containing hundreds of thousands of red bricks. These clays were greatly expanded in their uses particularly during the Georgian, Victorian and Edwardian eras to make the bricks, tiles and terracotta ornaments that created or adorn so many of Reading's buildings. The bricks and tile clays were originally all hand dug, shaped and moulded before being fired in a number of local kilns. Road names like Rose Kiln Lane are a reminder of this local handicraft that persisted for many centuries in and around the town.

Ice

c. 1 million years ago

Nobody knows for sure how the 'Ice Age' started, nor when it will end. There are several scientific theories that attempt to explain it but many stumble to fully explain *all* the observable facts. It is complex because the 'Ice' Ages consist of both 'cold' periods and interspersed  'warm' periods that alternate between arctic and sub-tropical conditions, and also that the geographical coverage of the ice sheets is substantially different in each of the recognisable cold periods.

The main theoretical contenders are: solar cooling when the amount of heat from the sun fluctuates, like someone fiddling with a central heating thermostat between hot and cold; polar wobbling which gives a geomagnetic twitch to the position of the north and south poles, where planetary ice is greatest, which would explain the differences in geographical coverage of ice sheets; or crustal shift theory, which postulates that (relatively) sudden movements of entire areas of the Earth's crust slipping over the underlying mantle thrust warm places towards the freezing cold poles. Currently, the main idea is the Milankovitch theory of atmospheric climate change.

There is no evidence that the massive two-mile-thick ice sheets ever reached the Reading area, stopping someway short of 'the Chilterns', but the effects of the cold (and the warm) periods would have been profoundly felt by any early residents of the 'Reading' area. At some point the 'Thames' cut through the chalk ridge and, instead of flowing out towards the North Sea and the now submerged landscape of 'Doggerland', took a southern path to create the Thames Valley much as we know it. An arctic tundra landscape was indicated during the cold periods where it was possible that nomadic peoples could have camped whilst hunting seasonal migrations of wildlife. The Chalk provided the raw material for knapping chunky flint hand axes and other crude implements possibly for chopping bones and meat. Some axes have been found in Reading associated with the Thames gravel terraces. These types of landscape would have been stark in the cold periods, subject to flash floods from glacial meltwater and as the ice sheets retreated, sea level changes would have impacted too. The 'Ice Age' deposited vast amounts of gravel that helped create some of the Reading landscapes we can see today. In the warmer inter-glacial periods the Thames Valley appeared to teem with archaic hippos, lions, hyenas and crocodiles like an African savannah landscape.

About 450,000 years ago rising sea levels first breached the chalk ridge barrier stretching from Kent to the Pas de Calais and created the Channel, cutting the land bridge for human communications between Britain and the European-Asian land mass. This was not the last breach (the land bridge reappeared and disappeared on other occasions) but the Channel, thereafter, has had a strong impact on the prehistoric and historic development of 'Reading' as a place inhabited by migrating peoples.

Palaeolithic Catastrophes

c. 12,900–10,600 years ago

Around 12,900 years ago the gently warming Northern Hemisphere and its thinly scattered human Palaeolithic inhabitants (modern humans and Neanderthals) appears to have suffered an extra-terrestrial catastrophe. The evidence for this is still being assessed but it created a debris field of tell-tale clues (nano-diamonds and a black mat of soot) from Alaska to Syria. The world was seemingly struck by fragments of a disintegrating comet that hit the two-mile thick North American ice-sheets near the Great Lakes with the equivalent force of 100 million nuclear warheads. At around 3000 degrees centigrade at impact this melted about one tenth of the ice, creating huge floods, super-hurricane blast winds, massive forest fires and the extinction of the northern mega-fauna. This theory

might explain why Ice Age mammoth corpses exhumed 'fresh' from the Siberian permafrost still have temperate grassland buttercups in their mouths (possibly due to displaced air from the impact creating a vacuum at ground level that was suddenly filled with freezing upper atmosphere air). Any of our ancestors passing through 'Reading' at the time would have been wiped out. A new mini Ice Age followed the impact, created by floods of very cold water into the Atlantic and sunlight-blocking clouds.

The trauma of the Palaeolithic past, however, was far from over. About 10,600 years ago it is thought that the comet trajectory (contained in the Taurids 'shooting stars' field) reconnected with Earth with possibly yet more airburst fragmentation (think of the Tunguska 1908 event but on a massive scale) or mega-tsunami oceanic impacts. These events probably de-glaciated the Northern hemisphere, ending the last Ice Age, and eventually raised global sea levels by c. 120 metres. This event might possibly be the source of the multiple human legends from cultures all over the globe that describe 'the flood'.

Did these Old Stone Age catastrophes lay waste to everything that was existing in the location of 'Reading', making it a clean slate a few centuries later for incoming migrants or survivors from elsewhere to begin again with a Middle Stone Age culture?

Mesolithic

c. 10,600 – 7000 years ago

There is a sharp change in Mesolithic times from bone-bashing chunky flint hand axes to thin flint blades and microliths. This might be because a completely new culture invaded the area or possibly that the late Palaeolithic mega-fauna and attendant humans had all been swept away. Clearly, from the nationally important flint tools and knapping remains found so far, particularly those in the Kennet Valley near 'Thatcham' and 'Newbury', a changeover took place in a relatively short time. People were still nomadic hunter-gatherers but in the Kennet Valley there were hints of settlement, possibly around non-migratory edible wild food or seasonal abundance. Evidence from Thatcham suggests that Mesolithic people ate pike, mallard, crane, goldeneye duck, hedgehog, water vole, hare, beaver, fox, pine martens, wildcat, red deer, roe deer and auroch. Elsewhere wild boars were eaten. Hazelnuts seem to have been an additional and important food as the climate warmed further.

Social coordination was required to hunt for types of food like deer or auroch using fire, perhaps at repeatedly used grazing or water access sites, to drive animals into killing zones. Other prey required skills such as fur trapping, fish trapping or archery.

The landscape around 'Reading' was transformed from the pine-aspen-birch woods of the late Palaeolithic to hazel followed by oak-elm-lime-alder. Contrary to the view that the chalk downs were open grassland, the evidence points to them being progressively wooded and people and animals converged on the more open floodplain margins of the braided river systems of the Thames and Kennet.

Neolithic

c. 7000–3800 years ago

The various peoples of the Neolithic, including the Wessex Beaker folk, have been described as the 'first farmers'. It seems that they may have worshipped the softly rounded chalk landscape as a living metaphor for the body of 'the mother' who provided them with nourishment, fertility, a place to commune with the ancestors and to see animistic spirits in everything from sky to soil. It was a long period of place making, wondering not wandering, and of cultivation rather than just following seasonal food abundances. The landscape around 'Reading' might have been marshy wetlands although near 'Sonning' the flat land was used to build an important parallel bank structure called a cursus, but nobody knows what purpose it served; another cursus has been found at Green Park. Woodland was being felled to make space for cultivation. Grazing was possibly practised on the drier, thin-soiled chalk downs. On the 'Berkshire

Downs' the great prehistoric trade route the Ridgeway met the Thames at 'Goring' and dotted along its route are Neolithic long barrows such as Wayland's Smithy or East Kennet.

The Kennet River might have been sacred to Neolithic people. Its source is close to Avebury in Wiltshire where the entire landscape seems to have been progressively filled with some of the most extraordinary sarsen stone and earthen ditch features *in the world*. The ditches were dug through 30 feet of chalk with deer antler picks to reach the water table and would fill up at the same time that the first gurgling bubbles of the young river surged out of the ground at Swallowhead. This spring is immediately adjacent to Silbury Hill, *the largest man-made prehistoric mound in Europe*. This is not accidental because a decorative water-filled moat was also created around the mound. Gravel from the Kennet formed the mound's first layer. Overlaying that were turves to create the base for the enormous heap of earth and chalk. Archaeologists found winged ants preserved in this foundation and, as these insects fly in late June, it is tantalising to think that it might have been Midsummer's Day when Silbury Hill was inaugurated. Our ancestors were obsessed with the passage of the stars and time. The 'hill' was a prodigious feat of terraforming. Its builders knew what they were doing (even if we don't know *why* they were doing it). The fact that it contains 500,000 tonnes of material means that it also took around 4 million man-hours just to emplace it, let alone a similar amount of time to dig it and the same again to transport it by the hod-load. These labouring humans would have needed yet more people to feed and accommodate them. It's possible that children and teenagers at summer tribal gatherings supervised by a few wise elders could have done all of this work. Perhaps that's something the 87,000 people attending Reading Festival could ponder on.

Bronze Age

c. 3800–2800 years ago

The theme of permanent farming that had begun in the Neolithic was consolidated in the Bronze Age. The juxtaposition of natural features that made the landscape around 'Reading' attractive to settlement, such as that beneath the current Green Park area, was being utilised. The rivers and ancient track-ways were transporting goods from near and far such as shale bracelets from Kimmeridge in Dorset and heavy quern-stones for grinding flour from Culham in Oxfordshire. The clays from the London Clay, the Reading Formation and river alluvium were being made into pots and continuously refined in terms of style, materials and applications. The chalk lands were being grazed by sheep, and cattle were being put out on the wetter pastures by the Thames and Kennet. Hunting for wild animals was still being carried out but probably to a much lesser degree and their bones do not form a large part of the remains found by archaeologists. Pigs are also mainly absent. Alongside these changes it is clear from the palynological records of pollen species that wetter woodland was being rapidly cleared away and there are many indications that large trees were being replaced by coppice woodland. Hazelnut remains are found in abundance; the kernels for food and the shells perhaps for fuel.

Although the metallurgical revolution called the Bronze Age was under way, in lower status agricultural settlements, flint was still the tool of choice and (much easier to cut) coppice wood was being burned. It might have been very smoky in places! Potters would need a lot of wood to fire their pots. Cooking, utilising flint nodules heated in wooden pyres and then placed in water-filled animal skins or sturdy pots to heat the water to cook the food (so called pot-boilers), would have taken a lot more wood. Great mounds of burnt and shattered flints are a feature

of this era but nobody knows precisely what activities they were from, although there are a number of theories. One of the suggestions is that they were from smoke saunas. These could have been constructed from cattle hides stretched over a wooden frame to make a crude dome in which flints were heated by log fires and then quenched with water to create the sauna steam. This might have started as a by-product of a method of tanning hides.

In more higher-status locations gold torcs, bracelets and beads would have been displayed and several examples of fine gold work, much of it originating from Ireland's gold mines, have been discovered in the Thames Valley, indicating a serious sea trade. The copper and tin minerals for bronze manufacture also had to be mined and smelted in Cornwall and then transported long distances.

Iron Age

c. 2800 years ago – 43 AD

Hallmstadt and Belgic Celts, Gauls, Franks, Britons; there are a range of names to describe the peoples who next invaded the island and overtook the Bronze Age tribal landscapes. They were certainly organised and war-like but also artistic and enjoyed a rich culture. The Celts seem to have emerged suddenly out of Scythia and spread throughout much of northern continental Europe. When this push reached the English Channel the Celts of Gaul and Germany crossed the water by boat to capture nearly the whole of Britain and divided it into tribal areas. The Gaulish Atrebates ruled around 'Reading' but had fiercer rivals across the Thames called the Catuvellauni (probably from Champagne), to the north-west the Dobunni and to the south west, the Belgae. 'Reading' was possibly an inland port for the tribal centre at modern Silchester. Here the Atrebates built a town with streets aligned to the mid-summer and mid-winter solstices. It must have been a special place for some reason because it eschewed close proximity to drinking water and the highway Thames.

Celtic Silchester had to rely on wells sunk into the underlying chalk for drinking supplies but was not short of luxury goods. There is evidence of extensive trade with Celtic Europe and Rome, particularly in iron weapons embellished with exquisite designs, and bronze, gold, copper, enamel, leather work, wine and food flavourings (and even olives) and with the coast for shellfish. Facilitating this trade apart from seaworthy boats was a network of track-

ways connecting the Celtic-Gaulish world to the Roman-Etruscan world further south. As landscape features that can be detected today the evidence for this pre-Roman road network is conjectural but temptingly argued for, as how otherwise would such sophisticated trade have taken place?

'Reading' at this time was likely to be a convenient transhipment point but there is no excavated evidence to support this idea. The river might then have been an uneasy neutral border between the Catuvellauni and the Atrebates. All that changed when Verica, the king of the Atrebates, sought Roman help to duff up his neighbours. Caractacus, one of the leaders of the Cats, ran him out of town, all the way to Rome. The Romans conveniently used this as a prompt for Claudius to invade. It sounds suspiciously like a WMD scam.

Romans

43–c. 410

It is probable that 'Reading' continued as a transhipment port for the Roman centre of occupation at Calleva Atrebatum (Silchester). The usefulness of a junction of two rivers at one of the narrowest parts of the Thames Valley could have allowed for wharfage and a main highway to the sea for bulky goods and provisions. Excavations at Newport in Wales and London have revealed that such ports with warehouses run by the military were well-established features of Roman life.

The Romans as 'Italian' military occupiers and migrant settlers soon set about transforming the landscape to their liking. Some of this was to clear out Celtic land use patterns in favour of Roman villa farming methods or to militarise Celtic towns by overlaying the preferred Roman cardinal point street orientations and gateways. This is apparent from Silchester where the Celtic street pattern has been discovered beneath the Roman layers.

The Roman landscape changes were probably mostly seen in the importation of new ideas to maintain the enjoyment of a higher standard of living. The Roman elites used the subjugated Atrebates as labour to grow and process crops (particularly grain), cut fuel wood for their hypocaust heating systems, maintain water supplies and supply the bricks, tiles and other building materials to create their forts and villas. The land-scape suddenly became much more organised, delineated and parcelled into new ownerships marked by roads and tracks leading from the great spine roads of the Roman Empire that criss-crossed the country. In Berkshire the Roman roads from Silchester led to Bath, Dorchester-on-Thames, Winchester, London and probably St Albans, and these were active trade routes that brought high quality red Samian ware pottery from Gaul, food and wines from the warmer parts of the Roman empire as well as exotic and decorative household goods. The palimpsest remnants of this communications infrastructure can still be seen today.

The Romans had it all, up to a point, but as with any arrogant usurper, the usurped sometimes fight back. There is evidence at Silchester that the Roman town was burnt to the ground at a time that loosely fits the date of the Boudiccan rebellion in the territory of the Iceni. Whether this act was Boudicca's personal handiwork or just copycat arsonists is unknown. Like all civil wars this could have had a devastating impact on the landscape around Reading through crop destruction, abandoned farms and displaced peoples.

Saxons

c. 410–871

In 410 AD the Roman occupation of Britannia began to dribble away as the seat of Empire came under attack from the pagan hordes north of the Alps. In Reading the Romano-Celtic mixed race nation must have been aware of the fragility of their security as the Roman armies departed and the Emperor Honorius sent back a stark message to the groaning Britons saying 'you're on your own pal'. Raids by Irish Scots, Picts and North Sea pirates using the tidal rivers like the Thames and Trent to penetrate inland became increasingly frequent from the North and East. The Romano-British reverted to the Celtic lifestyle of living in roundhouses and much of the Roman domestic infrastructure was gradually abandoned. The Romano-British tribal leaders like Vortigern sought to carry on the Roman practice of buying mercenary protection from the beefy Angles (North Holland-Schleswig-Holstein), Saxons (Germany) and Jutes (Jutland, Denmark) across the Channel but made the foolish error of welching on the deal. This led to some cross words and a number of massacres in Kent. It was then followed by successive waves of immigration into the south,

east and midlands by these militaristic, opportunistic and by now rather cross Germanic tribes.

Somewhere, amongst this unrecorded period in the fifth and sixth centuries, the long boats of Reada's people, of Sunna's folk and Woca's and Basa's people probably sailed and rowed up the Thames until they found a place they liked. Reada chose Reading; Sunna, Sonning; Woca, Wokingham; and Basa, Basingstoke. It is not entirely clear if the Romano-British tribes had all left to move westwards, emigrate to Brittany or Galicia or if they stayed to fight or assimilate as slaves at this time. The result, however, is very clear; the Anglo-Saxons intended to stay and mark their culture and practices upon the landscape. These cultural and land divisions are still felt today in their creation of names like Wessex (the land of the West Saxons) and even in the name of Ængland itself (the land of the Germanic Angles). They also used oxen to plough the heavy clays and introduced that most characteristic word of the English landscape, the field (feld) as well as minsters for churches. The pagans became Christianised and established minsters and burghs. Settled life in Saxon Ængland must have felt secure for at least 300 years but trouble was on the way. Some Anglo-Saxon words are still dominant in the language we use today especially when we are a bit annoyed.

Vikings

871–1066

The Viking 'presence' over here began in 793 with the pillage of Lindisfarne. This was religious revenge after the Frankish Christian 'Holy Roman Emperor' Charlemagne had started a war against the pagan Saxony Saxons in 772. Having subdued these Saxons the Danish Vikings anticipated that they would be next for forced baptisms or death. Prompted by this threat they decided to migrate; the Norwegian Vikings to Iceland, Ireland and Scotland, and the Danish Vikings to Ængland. The limit of the tidal Thames at this time was upstream of Staines, possibly near the Ankerwycke Yew opposite the Meadow of the Runes, so longboats could be pushed by the tides, sailed and then rowed deep into Saxon territory on sporadic probing raids. In 865 the Norwegians and Danes combined in the Great Heathen Army that invaded Britain and captured Thetford. From here it got serious.

The first historical mention of Reading as a place was on 4 January 871 when the Anglo-Saxon Chronicle relates that the Great Heathen Army's Danish Vikings camped their army at Kennetmouth and raised an earthen bank between Kennet and Thames to prevent assault from the west. Here the West Saxons led by their king and eorls unsuccessfully attacked. Later, the regrouped Saxons defeated the Danes at the Battle of Ashdown but lost the next two and their king. At this point Ælfred the Great took over kingship and paid off the Danes in gold. It was only a temporary fix but it gave Ælfred time to establish fortified burhs across his kingdom. The Danes returned in the late 870s but Ælfred eventually defeated King Guthrum at the Battle of Ethandun (Edington) in 878, leading to the treaty of 886 that 'peacefully' divided the country into Saxon and Danelaw counties. It lasted just over a century before Sweyn of Denmark invaded and Æthelred the Unready fled to Normandy. German-Danish Ængland and Reading was now totally Danish. Sweyn's son Canute then married Æthelred's widow Emma of Normandy. This raised Saxon hopes that Emma's first son Ædward, who became king, would produce a new Saxon dynasty. Wrong: he chose a vow of chastity instead and became Edward the Confessor, d'oh!

Normans

1066–1154

Did the dying Edward the Confessor promise old Anglo-Saxon-Danish 'Ængland' to the bastard Norwegian Viking William of Normandy? Did the Saxon aristocracy then double-cross William on the deal by crowning Harold Godwinson as their preferred candidate for the job and also annoy the King of Norway Harald Hardrada to boot? It could be put into the language of a boardroom struggle but when the takeover came it was bloody and brutal. There was the battle of Stamford Bridge. Not *that* Stamford Bridge. Then there was that *other* battle. The place of the battle became a sacred site to the conquerors, who built an abbey there in 1070 and the words Battle Abbey became attached to Reading's history because William gave confiscated Saxon-Danish estates in Reading for the upkeep of Battle Abbey in Sussex. There's a lovely copy of the Bayeux Tapestry in Reading Museum that tells this victor's view of the entire story, so go see it, and watch out for comets (and arrows).

William was so enraged by the Saxon duplicity after 1066 that he simply took the culture apart, erased all recognition of land ownerships of those who had fought against him at Hastings and confiscated titles, attacked any parts of the Saxon shires that resisted, murdered the resistance and laid waste to the landscape. It was brutal and, having burnt their boats on the beach at Pevensey, the Normans were here to stay building motte and bailey castles in the wake of their rampages and installing loyal Norman over-lords to suppress the flaxen Saxons. However, William wasn't that interested in Ængland really, just the loot, and allowed important Saxons who could be useful to retain their estates but left Odo

the battling bishop, his half brother, in charge and soon scuttled back to Normandy to consolidate his continental powerbase.

In Reading the key river crossing and communication junction may have merited a motte to ensure that any tolls to be extracted or rebellions to quell could be done so quickly, but there is no proof of it. Stephen built a stone castle on a mound here in 1150 but demolished it in 1152 during the Anarchy. It was used again in the seventeenth century and is now known as 'Forbury Hill'. Raising cash required an audit of everything valuable so that the fat could be skimmed off the kingdom. The Domesday survey of 1086 was a prodigious undertaking but allowed William to asset-strip an entire country with military efficiency. In Reading six watermills were recorded, four on land belonging to the king and two belonging to Battle Abbey.

Henry I

1100–1135

It could be argued that Henry I was the man who made Reading. He certainly put it on the map and continues to excite morbid interest. However, he was a complex character mix of vision, viciousness and vitality. As a landless royal beneath his elder brothers William (Rufus) and Robert in the inheritance pecking order he needed other interests. He was therefore not unused to tossing captive opponents off towers and had enough sexual energy to father three legitimate children and 22 bastards. It seems probable that he participated in a *coup d'état* by murdering his brother Rufus in the New Forest in 1100. Leaving King Rufus to rot in the bushes, he rushed to Winchester to bag the royal treasury and thence a quickie coronation in Westminster. This was followed by a speedy political marriage to Matilda, the daughter of the King of Scotland, but also a descendant of Ælfred the Great. This was intended to gain favour from both Norman-French and Saxon-Danish nobilities. He imprisoned his elder brother Robert for life.

The landscape of Reading was graced during Henry I's reign with a major addition that has shaped it ever since. Strangely, it owes its origins to a small piece of French coastal landscape, a semi-submerged rock called the 'Quillebœuf' off the coast at Barfleur. Here, on the night of 25 November 1120, the White Ship (La Blanche-Nef) with 300 crew and passengers was wrecked. The evidence seems to indicate that the crew and many noble passengers, including Henry's only surviving legitimate son and successor William Adelin, had been drinking excessively (or had their drink spiked) and the

50 befuddled rowers took a short cut out of Barfleur harbour, drove the ship onto the rock and all except a butcher from Rouen were drowned. Henry collapsed on hearing the news and his dashed plans for succession. As a result of this grief Henry turned to God and in 1121 ordered that the Cluniacs from Burgundy should be given the important site between the Kennet and Thames to found Reading Abbey. It was a huge undertaking and was partly designed to host Henry's burgeoning collection of holy relics. Henry handed over all his interests in Reading to the Abbot in 1125, who then became its principal controller. Whether or not the wrecking of the White Ship was 'an accident' or pre-meditated mass-murder is still open. 'Cui bono', who might gain from such a tragedy? There was one such person who suspiciously left the boat just before it sailed complaining of 'diarrhoea'. A man called Stephen of Blois. After the death of Henry I in 1135 and before Reading Abbey was completed, Stephen declared himself king of England and started the vicious civil war called 'the Anarchy' with Henry's daughter Matilda of Anjou.

Ecclesiastic Landscapes and Pilgrim Trails

Reading Abbey rose slowly from its gravelly foundations and took from 1125 to 1164 to complete. Henry I had endowed it with lands and an impressive collection of holy relics bought, acquired or filched on his warring travels. After his death in Rouen in December 1135 his gralloched cadaver was transported to Reading sewn into an ox-hide to be buried there before the altar of the incomplete abbey in January 1136. In June 2016 work began with ground-penetrating radar to establish if the remains of Henry and his queens could be rediscovered. There is a hunch that it will be under a car park, possibly beneath parking space H1.

Henry's influence lived on through his endowments. The list of holy relics that created such a lucrative pilgrim industry for the monks is impressive. Chief amongst the treasures was the foreskin or prepuce of Jesus Christ, previously in the possession of the Emperor Constantine. After that came bottles of blood and water from Jesus at the crucifixion, a piece of his shoe and some stones and dirt from Bethlehem. Some of the BVM's hair and parts of her bed mingled with Aaron and Moses' rods, manna from Mount Sinai and even part of the rock that Moses struck. There was the hand of St James and a number of bony parts of several saints including Simeon, Thomas, Luke, Andrew, Philip, Mary Magdalene,

Pancras, Quinton, David Eadward the martyr, Jerome, Stephen, Blaise, Osmund, Aethelwold, Leodegarius, Herefrith, Margaret, Arnulf, Agnes, Frideswide and Anne.

A new landscape connection thenceforth emerges with the hundreds of thousands of pilgrims that were to be found wandering around Europe seeking miracles, blessings or cures, spiritual clarity or a reassured passage to the Afterlife through sin atonement. Reading Abbey was up there with Santiago di Compostela, and Walsingham, on the travel agents' map of pilgrimage hotspots if long haul to the Holy Land or Rome was unavailable. The link to Santiago through the blessed hand of St James was strong and the motif of these pilgrims, the scallop shell, is still found on the University of Reading logo.

Pilgrims at Reading Abbey were offered two nights B & B free with an option to stay longer if you paid and could cope with the bed bugs. The Hospitaller of the Cluniacs organised this *c.* 400-bed 'hotel' and secured the food and other supplies that the pilgrims needed from the Reading hinterland. Scraps of leftover pilgrim food, 'orts', were offered to local beggars, a word still connected to Reading in Orts Road. The sale of overpriced votive candles, pilgrimage tokens and trinkets as well as gifts became a big source of income and the Cluniac monks expanded their wealth as a result but irritated the rising class of merchant traders.

Wool and Cloth

Between 1250 and 1550 the economic activity of sheep grazing in England, including the hinterlands of Reading, increased and cloth manufacturing boomed. The landscape impacts of this wealth creation were enormous.

Wool had always been used to spin and weave and loom weights have been discovered in archaeological digs from the Bronze Age onwards. The critical changes were the introduction of fluffier sheep from the Mediterranean countries and less use of the coarser fibres of native sheep. In landscape terms the chalk downs around Reading became extensively used for sheep rather than cattle and lowland pastures became enclosed to prevent sheep wandering into arable fields. Tree cover and shrubs were cleared to increase the profitability of these lands and a cadre of shepherds was employed to protect these valuable flocks.

In the early medieval period the main trade was in raw wool exports to London, thence to Flanders and the rest of Europe where it was made into cloth. The woolsack became a symbol of new wealth and the Speaker of the House of Lords still sits on 'the woolsack' although there is also a larger woolsack called the Judges' Woolsack that any member can sit on. In the later medieval period, however, particularly after the ravages of the Black Death in 1349, raw wool exports fell but after a short interval of social recovery sales of cloth made in England simultaneously increased as the added value inherent in cloth was exploited. This demanded a whole host of new trades that impacted upon the landscape. Fast flowing rivers to wash and pound the wool fibres using water wheels fitted to crude camshaft hammers were needed. The multi-stranded Kennet at Reading's 'seven bridges' proved to be eminently suitable for this activity. Dyes were made from plants such as woad, saffron, madder, elderberry, lichens or oak galls. Saffron crocus bulbs were planted at Inkpen and were believed to have originated via the Knights 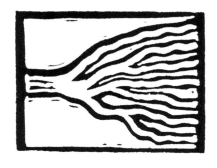 Templar returning from the Mediterranean. Mordants such as alum (hydrated potassium aluminium sulphate) had to be mined as shale, burnt and slaked with seaweed and stale urine. When Henry VIII was excommunicated by the Pope imports of alum ceased and the only domestic source was Ravenscar on the Yorkshire coast. Burning one hundred foot high piles of alum shale here irretrievably devastated the coastal landscape. To take the grease out of the wool, Fuller's Earth, a smectite formed from volcanic ash deposited in seawater, was dug from Jurassic-age Lower Greensand rocks in the Cotswolds and brought to the fulling mills. Teasels were collected by the tens of thousands to help card the wool fibres into straightened lengths for easier spinning. The landscape was alive with wool-related activities and the town with working people.

In Reading, and surrounding towns such as Newbury where John Winchcombe was prominent, new trade centres for woollen cloth manufacture and Guilds to represent their commercial interests rapidly developed but clashed with the Abbot who controlled the markets.

Welsh Tudors and Dissolution

1485–1558

Edmund Tudor begat Henry VII who claimed the throne through the Battle of Bosworth; he in turn, had four children with Welsh ancestry including the man who became Henry VIII in 1509. Henry VII had promised the Pope that Henry VIII would marry Catherine of Aragon (Henry VIII's dead elder brother Arthur's widow) who was geopolitically convenient as the very Catholic daughter of the very Catholic King of Spain. It was a European union that kept the faith. Henry VIII disagreed and kicked off. In short order he was ex-communicated by the Pope, founded his own religion and murdered a lot of his wives.

The consequences for Reading's principal landscape feature, the Abbey, were disastrous. There had been popular resentment against the wealth of the Catholic establishment at a time of widespread poverty for many years. Henry wanted cash and saw the church as a convenient cashpoint to plunder. He despatched his secretary Thomas Cromwell to find out what he could make by dissolving the monasteries and in 1538 a sympathetic Parliament approved the process. In September, Dr John London, one of Cromwell's commissioners, looted the BVM's pilgrims shrine at Caversham, trashed Greyfriars and set about preparing for the removal of the goodies from Reading Abbey with the connivance of Thomas Vachell, MP for Reading. Dr John, however, was most indignant when the poor of Reading rushed in to remove what was left at Greyfriars; 'most things that might be had they stole away, in so much that they had conveyed the very clappers of the bells.' Rich stuff from a royal

looter. The Abbey struggled on for a year before the bells tolled its death knell and the barbaric public execution of its last abbot in November 1539. The buildings were taken over as a royal residence and the merchants of Reading at last took over the running of the town using the conveniently empty Greyfriars as their new Guildhall. After Henry's death in 1547 the Duke of Somerset arrived to finish the job of looting what was left and began demolishing the abbey itself. Much of the stone, lead and timber was flogged off to London on barges and some used to restore buildings in Reading including St Mary's Church, which paid 6s. 8d. for 21 loads of timber. The dodgy Duke made even bigger sums in London flogging all the old glass for just over £6 and another £6 from Reading's avaricious MP for the entire roof of the Abbey library. The lucrative pilgrim trade stopped, the alleged blessed hand of St James was secretly hidden and most of Reading's most visible asset simply vanished.

Elizabethan Reading

1558–1603

Fashion, private wealth and public poverty developed strongly under the Tudors. Trade in woollen products was one of the key ingredients for the success of Reading and the surrounding areas; mercers such as Reading's John Kendrick (who left £30,000 in his will when he died in 1624) made fortunes but Elizabeth I inherited a dilapidating national cloth industry. Reading was also getting dilapidated, with nineteen bridges in need of urgent repair. The royal charter granted to Reading by good Queen Bess consolidated the power of the burghers and merchants (and gave them a new town hall) but also commanded that 30 oak trees from Whitley along with another 200 cartloads of stone from the remains of the Abbey were to be used to make good the bridges. Its three parish churches now afforded Reading's most remarkable presence in the landscape but even these were not left unmolested by the new religion. All the churches were stripped of any whiff of Catholicism; all the stained glass replaced by plain and medieval frescoes whitewashed.

Throughout England and in the landscape around Reading, bad harvests led to a famine in 1586 and some of this was put down to the use of good agricultural land for woad production for the cloth dyers. Royal proclamations of 1585 and 1587 sought to regulate its growth within four miles of a market or clothing town and limits of 60 acres in any one parish or 20 acres by one grower. Cloth was still seen as a national icon and the Elizabethan sea-faring explorer-coloniser-privateer-entrepreneurs such as Raleigh were using English cloth as a trade gift in their dealings with bemused Native Americans in places like Roanoke.

The wealthy got wealthier and the poor got poorer. Huge brick mansions were erected at places such as Englefield and Mapledurham but later workhouses like Kendrick's 'Oracle' (built in 1628) were created in Reading to do the job that the Abbey used to do in looking after the impoverished and sick. Whipping the idle became an Elizabethan profession and the cost of looking after the vagrants and infirm fell upon the indignant local government worthies. Welcome to the welfare state.

The three Parishes of **Reading** in the seventeenth century

St Laurence's

St Mary's

ABBEY RUINS

FRIAR STREET

BROAD STREET

CASTLE ST.

SEVEN BRIDGES

MILL LANE

LONDON ST.

St Giles'

Kennet

town population c.5000

Civil War, Republicanism and Restoration

1603–1714

Taxes, fines, violent appropriations, unpaid loans, stolen food, broken bridges, commandeered supplies, trade curtailed and civilians turned into defence ditch-diggers were just a taste of the impact of the Civil War on Reading almost before battle had commenced. Ruinous changes to the urban landscape of Reading affected the town's economy for decades. The violence of siege and counter-attack knocked the stuffing out of the townscape, its most prominent buildings and the landscape for miles around. All the farm workhorses were stolen and anything that was not nailed down was nicked by hungry, cold and disgruntled troops of both sides in the bitter dispute between King and Parliament.

Reading stood inconveniently at the crossroads of war, King Charles at Oxford and Parliament at Windsor with the Thames as a transport route between them. Charles I trundled into town on 3 November 1642 after abandoning London. His attitude was the divine right of kings personified but he was also broke and demanded that the townspeople feed and garrison his troops, supply new clothing, horse-fodder and stump up £4000 in cash. His army set the town up for a siege by Parliamentary forces that duly arrived in April 1643. Reading was strenuously attacked with cannon and musket fire and badly damaged.

Charles managed to retreat to Oxford and the roundheads arrived to find the place in pieces but 'not ill-stored with provisions [...] plenty of beer and wines [...] meat, oats and wheat'. Most of these troops stayed just six weeks until the food ran out when Royalists reoccupied the town. In May 1644 the Royalists were attacked by the Parliamentary troops in a second siege, intent on starving them out if they couldn't shoot them out. Many properties, especially church towers used as gun emplacements, were demolished by cannon-fire. Eventually a surrender was negotiated just as a chastened Charles arrived from Oxford to lift the siege. The cavaliers departed and the roundheads reoccupied what was left of the ruined town until the end of the war.

After Charles was captured he briefly returned to Caversham under guard and was allowed to meet his children at Maidenhead before being prepared for trial. The Civil War had split asunder Reading's property-owning families like the Vachells and the Blagraves; indeed Daniel Blagrave became a signatory to the death warrant of Charles I leading to the beheading in 1649. Reading and the rest of England became a republic and commonwealth.

The effects of the civil war lingered and 'hardly a sheep, hen, hog, oats, hay, wheat or any other thing' remained abroad in the landscape.

It took more that the restoration of Charles II and gossip about his profligate lifestyle 'Restless he rolls from whore to whore. A merry monarch, scandalous and poor' to bring any cheer to the inhabitants, their disarrayed trades and shattered buildings.

Dutch Bloodless Orange Revolution

1688

The ruination of Reading's principal trades in the 1640s was compounded both by the corruption of Charles II in the 1660s and the return of Catholicism with James II in the 1680s. Reading was an independent-thinking place in matters of religion but when Charles's Uniformity Act outlawed these opinions their proponents often went

abroad. The Quakers, however, often went to Reading Gaol. Admiral William Penn was not one of them but his son William Penn, who later lived and died near Reading in Ruscombe, was a Quaker and instrumental not only in creating the intellectual foundations of the United States of America but also the European Parliament. Admiral Penn brought Charles II back for his restoration and also gave him the equivalent of £2.25 million in loans. After his death these favours were used in a deal with his dissident son in exchange for 45,000 square miles of land in North America. In return he had to write off the loan and rid England of as many Quaker families as possible. The name chosen by Penn was 'Sylvania' but Charles altered the Charter in 1681 to Pennsylvania to honour Penn's father: in 1748 the town of Reading, Berkshire County was established there.

The landscapes of battle are usually ruinous but in 1688 Reading (England) took one for the team and the only fighting of the whole 'Bloodless Revolution' took place in the town centre and occupied a mere few hours. After William of Orange had landed his Dutch troops at Brixham, King James sent Irish troops to Reading to block any advance on London. Fearing that they might be massacred, the townspeople sent a runner to Hungerford where William was camped at the Bear Hotel to seek help. On 9 December William sent the Duke of Nassau with 650 troops to take Reading. Sneaking in from the Pangbourne side they surprised the Irish in the town centre and routed them with a cavalry charge in Market Place. Leaving their dead behind, the Irish troops fled to the Loddon at Twyford pursued by 50 Dutch cavalry. The war was over.

The re-restoration of a Protestant leadership with William and Mary created the Toleration Act allowing persecuted sects to worship alongside state religion, adding to the Reading townscape many places of non-conformist worship. After the Dutch rulers of England died, the corpulent Queen Anne, chided by the Act of Settlement of 1701, had 17 pregnancies but left no *Protestant* survivors. The Act had fixed it (and is still law) that only non-Catholics could rule, so despite 56 closer Catholic successors, the newly created United Kingdom had to look through the 'P for Protestant' section of the Argos catalogue of European Royalty to find a French-speaking German, Georg Ludwig, to rule Britannia.

German Georgians

1714–1759

The news that 'George 1' would be popping over from Hannover to rule the UK led to rioting in over twenty Great British towns including Reading. However, these were Tory riots organised by the High Anglicans and were targeted at Reading's growing population of non-conformists, whose attackers cried 'No Hanover, no Cadogan, but Calvert and Clarges!', the latter two names being those of Reading's Tory MPs. These disturbances led to the creation of the Riot Act of 1715.

When not filled with rioting Tories the streets of Reading took on a new feel under the Georgians, with the addition of many new buildings built with local bricks. Although tiles and bricks had been made since Roman times they were more expensive than timber with wattle and daub infill. Reading was overlooked by that wooded hill where tiles were made, Tilehurst, and custom-made bricks were made for specific buildings throughout the medieval period. The Georgians made it an industry and Reading had a sufficiency of raw materials to make very red bricks (the famous 'Reading Reds') as well as yellow ones from the London Clay and whitish or purplish ones when chalk was added. The chalk was directly mined beneath Reading close to the kilns. As well as Tilehurst, kilns were established at Calcot, Caversham, Katesgrove and Coley alongside other geological outliers at Wargrave, Ruscombe and Knowl Hill to the east. Clay was dug in the winter to weather and reduce moisture and under later law could only be fired between March and October. It was admixed with chalk or sand in a pug-mill before moulding and firing. The kilns themselves were crude affairs at first with piles of bricks covered by fuel wood and turf, but grew more sophisticated

as demand increased and bespoke brick dome kilns had to be constructed. The landscape was transformed by clay workings, brickyards and nearby woodlands denuded of trees. Smoke filled the air during the firing season.

By the nineteenth century large-scale brick-making companies such as S&E Collier were buying up the smaller specialist companies such as Katesgrove's Waterloo Kiln founded by John Poulton and Samuel Wheeler's chimney pot firm of Tilehurst Potteries at Kentwood Hill. Many firms struggled into the Edwardian era and beyond but could not compete with the huge manufactures around Peterborough and Bedford. Prospect Park Kiln was the last to go. Many of Reading's finest remaining buildings from these eras, such as Alfred Waterhouse's Town Hall, are built from the most local of Reading's local landscape-related materials; a fact recognised by Thomas Hardy when he used the term for old brick town, 'Aldbrickham' as the name to describe Reading in his book *Jude the Obscure*, published in 1895.

Farmer George and 'the Rural War'

1760–1838

George III was the first of the German (Hanoverian) migrant kings to be born in England (reigned 1760–1820) but was keen to do humble things like pig-rearing and show how 'British' he really was. However, he actively lost the 'British' colonies in America although was more successful in helping to win the Battle of Trafalgar using Katesgrove-made sailcloth in 1805 and defeating Napoleon at the Battle of Waterloo in 1815, despite by then being blind, deaf and demented. The obese, adulterous, bigamist George IV who had been acting as Regent for some time succeeded George v3. The Duke of Wellington had a few choice words to describe him and his wastrel ways. These events and others had a bearing on life in Reading and its surrounding agricultural hinterland. Much of this was due to increasing land values, enclosure of commons and lost commoner 'cottage' economies, new rural technology, worsening agricultural wages, the Speenhamland Declaration and the rising price of bread. Yeoman farmers and landed estates did well under the Georges but were less willing to pay for the relief of poverty amongst their farmworkers and jobless parishioners. William IV was recruited as King in 1830 at the ripe age of 64 having already settled into domestic bliss in Bushy Park with 'Mrs Jordan' and their ten illegitimate children (to whom David Cameron is related).

It was a time of revolution and establishment fear. William Cobbett called the 1830–31 period 'the Rural War', otherwise called the 'Swing Riots', and frequently passed through Reading on his rural rides raging at Parliament, 'tax-eaters' and tea-drinkers in equal, seditious measure. In the agricultural fields and villages surrounding Reading, starving and impecunious agricultural labourers were burning hayricks, smashing threshing machines and threatening farmers and clergy for money to survive the winter. The Government's response in Berkshire, on Christmas Day 1830, was to assemble 300 troops to arrest the ringleaders and send them to Reading Gaol. The summary Reading Court judgements against the 138 prisoners resulted in 23 being sentenced to death and the rest to transportation to Australia or imprisonment. William Winterbourne of Kintbury was immediately executed at Reading Gaol on 11 January 1831 pleading to the end that his wife, who was seriously ill with typhus, might die before she heard of his fate. The taste of beer and biscuits would thenceforth be slightly bitter.

Canal Fever

In 1702 Queen Anne had taken a fancy to Bath where she became convinced that the sulphur-stinky thermal waters of *Aquae Sulis* would be good for her. This smelly new fashion required new infrastructure and soon the London to Bath coach road through Reading previously mainly used by plodding carthorses was gentrified by courtly people who wanted 'better everything'. Horses had to be changed every ten miles or so, inns improved and this regal relay race made those suppliers on the route suddenly prosperous. For goods it was different as packhorse trains and carts were ponderously slow. Barge traffic was the answer.

Ever since those with the wits to see the possibilities of creating a safe, non-sea route between London and Bristol first put pen to parchment has the idea of a canal been considered. Sea traffic around Land's End was hazardous and ships, lives and valuable cargoes were frequently lost. As an adjunct to the industrialisation of natural products a calm, inland waterway ticked all the boxes amidst the chattering industrial revolutionaries of the seventeenth and eighteenth centuries. So, the idea to link the wiggly rivers of Avon and Kennet was first considered just after the English Civil War. The intractable violent opposition of landowners and more importantly water mill owners delayed the development of the

idea for a canalised river to get boats up the Kennet until 1723, when the short cut to Newbury was built with 20 locks. This allowed coal up from London and bulk agricultural produce from the landscapes around Reading to flow eastwards at a fraction of the previous cost. By 1794 the canal link to Bristol via the Kennet and Avon Canal was commenced and completed in 1810. The Thames was also improved with pound locks and the new Oxford Canal brought even cheaper coal, iron and ceramics from the newly industrialised Midlands.

Although the majority of the directly impactful landscape changes from contour-following canal building such as the great aqueducts, tunnels, locks, staircase locks and cuttings were not seen in Reading it was important as a centre of wharfage and transhipment. Everyone wanted cheaper bulk good deliveries and safer exports of Reading's many new products. The oceanic port cities of London and Bristol were now Reading's gateway to the rest of the world.

Railway Mania

1838–1901

HRH Alexandrina Victoria of Kent's ascension to the throne in 1838 neatly coincided with the arrival of the railways in Reading. Things were about to get a whole lot faster, dirtier and industrial. The migrants in charge were still German but trying not to be quite so German. The installation of the spruce fir Christmas tree, a particularly Teutonic pagan totem, by Prince Albert might not have been to everyone's taste but it gradually caught on. Fuel for the industrial revolution, however, was based not on wood but coal and the railways being both fuelled by coal and carrying the coals created massive changes in the rural and urban landscapes of Reading. The legacy of coal gas manufacture gave the Reading rail-side skyline its impressive (but now depleted) shape-shifting gasometers.

The Great Western Railway Company was established in 1833 and instructed Isambard Kingdom Brunel to survey a level as possible route to link London and Bristol. However it wasn't until February 1836 that construction began but had only reached Twyford by 1839. The great cutting at Sonning, with vast amounts of spoil to be dug out by hand and tipped to create the embankments leading to Reading station, occupied nearly three years of arduous and, on occasions, lethal work by the army of navvies. These poorly-skilled but hard-working men were soon to be seen chopping, digging and tunnelling the route westwards to Bristol to lay the tracks to link with Brunel's other dream, the massive trans-Atlantic paddle-steamer the Great Eastern. In March 1840 the first train from London reached Reading Station and, the following year, Bristol, much to the delight of its merchants. Less delightful for carpenter Henry West was the tornado that struck the station on 24 March 1840 and carried him to his doom along with the roof lantern; a lethal reminder that the location and topography of Reading puts it firmly at the centre of southern England's tornado alley.

Railway mania was soon in full swing and Reading became an attraction for both GWR expansion as well as other railway companies, with lines connecting to London Waterloo, Guildford, Basingstoke, Newbury and Oxford. Each one of these lines had a massive impact on the urban infrastructure of Reading with bridges, viaducts and cuttings, and the previous tranquillity of its rural hinterland. The railways were a game-changer for all commercial activity as speed of goods could now be measured in hours and not days or weeks taken by road users or the horse-drawn barges. Opportunists like Martin Hope Sutton and George Palmer immediately saw the massive potential that the railways had for their businesses and exploited it to the fullest degree.

Beer Bonanza

The agricultural landscapes around Reading once dominated by sheep were growing crops such as barley by the late eighteenth century. This was being transformed into malt for shipment to London using the Thames and Kennet's largest barges. However, as with wool and cloth before it, the added value of beer-making in Reading began to make economic sense and William Simonds developed beer production alongside his main malting business using barley from the family estates near Hurst and Arborfield. The onset of the Napoleonic Wars (thirsty soldiery) and lucrative contracts to supply the Royal Military Academy at Sandhurst and later the Brtish Army at Aldershot gave his son William Blackall Simonds, who inherited the business in 1782, the commercial break he needed to expand his small town brewery in Broad Street into something much bigger. It eventually developed India Pale Ale for export to the British Army in India and outlets in garrison countries such as Gibraltar and Malta. He was in the right place at the right time. Sir John Soane designed Simonds a model brewery (steam-powered from 1799) on the banks of the Kennet near County Lock in 1790 so that raw materials could be more easily imported and beer exported. Rebuilt in 1900, it remained there as the Seven Bridges Brewery until 1978.

WB was also interested in banking, both as a means to use the cash his publicans passed to him daily but also as a future security if beer drinking went out of fashion or was curtailed by social movements like Temperance. Until the passing of the Beerhouse Act of 1830 no new public houses were allowed and most of the local populace used brewhouses. This was an era when 'small beer' (low alcohol content) was a safer (bacterial) option than public pumps or communal well water. The ingredients of small beer were cheap, plentiful and easily obtainable, including wild plants such as ale hoof or fuggles to clarify the drink.

Key to commercial beer production in Reading was a good water supply, a deep well into the chalk bedrock beneath the brewery, malted barley from local grain fields and a touch of that 'pernicious weed', as hops were called when first introduced, and which formed the trade mark motif on every bottle of Simonds beer (and can be seen on the still existing Maltese variant today). Thus Simonds Brewery found itself in a growing town on a railway, plentiful supplies of the raw ingredients and huge contracts not only with the British Army but also most of the southern railway companies. It was taken over by Courage in the 1960s, briefly moved to giant brain-boggling vertical stainless steel tanks near the M4 and then wiped off the face of the Earth in 2010. The last swallow of a long summer of beer.

Cocks's Sauce

Cocks's Sauce was known as the King of Sauces, also as Reading Sauce, but by the end of Victoria's reign it had been out-competed by upstart Lea & Perrins' Worcestershire Sauce. The cheek of it – the saucy Worcester monkeys!

Reading Sauce was famous just about everywhere that the British Empire reached and even French writer Jules Verne captured its essence in 1872 as a mention in 'Around the World in Eighty Days'. This was long before product placement but emphasised the point that even such humble condiments as a bottle of sauce could become a global item of trade.

The sauce itself was 'commoditised' by Mr Cocks and made by Mrs Cocks. The Reading Sauce empire lasted from initial experimental products in 1789 at the Cocks's fishmongers shop all the way to 1962 before popping its cork for the last time. The final factory site was in the spot now occupied by the Reading Central Library and surely deserves some public art commemoration lest Reading totally forgets this largely forgotten historic sauciness.

Reading Sauce manufacture had an impact on the local landscape as the main ingredient was walnut ketchup made from green walnuts. Although limited quantities of green walnuts could have been obtained at the outset around Reading, where there are many fine trees still in existence, it seems unlikely that the volumes required at peak production would have been all local. The other ingredients, such as mushroom ketchup, were handpicked locally as field and horse mushrooms (*Agaricus campestris* and *Agaricus arvensis*). Imported from afar were the other constituents; chillies, garlic, salt, soy from India and somewhat improbably anchovies all the way from the Black Sea.

The ingredients were packed away in second-hand barrels from Simonds brewery and marinated for at least five years before being rolled out. A sauce upon which the sun never set for nearly 200 years; you've got to admire it.

Empire of Biscuits

Queen Victoria became Empress of India in 1876 after the Indian Mutiny of 1857 when the state took over the private-armied, drug-pushing enterprise the British East India Company (EIC). There was a two-way impact from the looting of India. Firstly, the fortunes created by exploitation of the Indian peoples were brought back to England and financed the establishment of some of the estates and grand houses in Berkshire, including Basildon Park and the re-furbishment of the Englefield Estate. Many of the owners, dubbed the 'Nabobs', clustered around the Hanoverian royals at Windsor Castle. William Pitt, later to become Prime Minister, was an EIC operator, diamond smuggler and tax-evader. His estate at Swallowfield and others near Reading made huge changes in the countryside as the money from India was spent lavishly on the new fad for romantic landscape architecture. Secondly, the exportation of goods from Berkshire and Reading grew spectacularly with the stimulus of imperial markets.

The industrialisation of Reading's manufacturing companies stepped up a gear and the town's character changed with it. Huntley and Palmers' biscuits and many other products saw their way to the furthest reaches of the British Empire, conveyed by canal, river, rail and steamship. All these aspects brought big changes in the land-scapes of supply as well as in the Reading townscape of production. Huntley (and later Palmer) had begun as a two-man bakery in 1822 selling loose biscuits to stage coach passengers but grew, by the end of the century, to become the biggest biscuit manufacturer in the world. It was George Palmer who had the vision to engage in mecha-nisation and worked with local iron-maker William Exall to invent a rolling oven biscuit machine. In 1846 the factory moved adjacent

to the canal and the railway and simply continued to grow, as biscuits became a fashionable aspect of taking afternoon tea. Queen Victoria took a fancy to their fancies and soon H & P was 'by appointment'. The company fast became Reading's largest employer and created a massive feature in the townscape with brick chimneys, railway yards, the 'biscuit tunnel' and required terraced houses for its workers; and rural landscape impacts too as agricultural suppliers strove to keep up with demand. H & P soon outgrew Swallowfield and Sonning mills and began importing flour from East Anglia. Belgium, Ireland, Barbados, France and Spain became suppliers of ingredients like eggs, sugar, coconuts and butter in prodigious quantities. Exports, in the wonderful tins made by Huntley, Boorne and Stevens in Reading, were despatched from 1868 to every corner of the biscuit-munching globe after the invention of offset-litho printing. These tins had their own landscape impacts, with tin from Cornwall and elsewhere in the Empire, smelted in South Wales to make tin plate using Welsh coal; there, parts of the landscape are still so toxic that grass cannot grow.

Landscapes of Leisure

1901–1914

After the funereal end to the Victorian Age the need for a brighter new century seemed to infect the populace. It lasted a little over a decade but new artistic freedoms that had been held in check by the dark side of Victoria's prolonged mourning emerged in *fin de siècle* Art Nouveau and found general expression in leisure and frippery. Some of this new century elation was expressed in exotic Reading terracotta tiles and brick ornamentation as well as gardening and some of it messing about in boats; all of which found a home in Reading or alongside and on the River Thames.

The rise of Suttons Seeds, utilising the river's deposit account of former floods of alluvium, a mixture of silt and humus, in the former gardens of the abbey at the back of the Market Place, was

good for Reading. Like other industries in the town, the railways gave Suttons Seeds an advantage in fast despatch and created happy gardeners treating their allotments to a string of Ailsa Craig onions (from 1887) or fluffing out their herbaceous borders with delightful floral bulbs. The introduction of the new Uniform Penny Post in 1840 was a huge breakthrough moment for seed sales. It was also another era of varieties and horticultural innovations, of public parks

bedecked with floral clocks and other aspects of vegetable pride. People wanted quality unadulterated seeds and Suttons was adroitly placed to both feed this demand and guarantee it. The Royal Seed Establishment as established by entrepreneur Martin Hope Sutton expanded to fill a huge, six-acre area of Reading and soon became the biggest in the world. The new growing areas were sited so that train passengers could see their floral glory as they passed as a living billboard in the landscape.

Prospect Park was acquired by Reading Corporation in 1901 and Forbury Gardens, first fully opened as a public park in 1860, continued to be used for public recreation and leisure pursuits. It is the setting for the Maiwand Lion, one of the world's largest iron sculptures, recording the deaths of 286 soldiers in the Royal Berkshire Regiment fighting in the Second Afghan War in 1880. Caversham was annexed in 1911 in a less bloody raid on Oxfordshire.

World War I and Inter-War Years

1914–1938

The landscape of Reading was not turned into a morass of death and muddy struggle, unlike the places on the front line in France and Belgium. It emerged unscathed, albeit beset with thousands of wounded soldiers from the 1914–18 conflict and Irish prisoners from the 1916 Dublin Easter Uprising.

In 1919 the Co-operative Wholesale Society commenced production at its national jam, canned fruit and pickles factory at Coley. The Jam Factory, as it was affectionately called, was sandwiched between the Holy Brook and the Kennet and used the old canal wharves as well as the GWR goods railway line to transport fruit and its products. Every Co-op shop in the UK was supplied from Reading. It became a major, if sticky, employer, utilised 48 giant jam pans and, at its peak, was filling and distributing 1.7 million jars of jam a year.

In the 1920s the riverscape changed dramatically with the construction of two new bridges over the Thames, to take the increasing

amount of traffic, and newly laid out riverside parks and promenades between and around them.

New council housing estates such as Whitley and private ones were developed to cope with population growth and renew old stock. Southcote, Calcot Park, Coley Park, Maiden Erleigh, Erleigh Court and Caversham Park were all sold by their owners during the inter-war years and converted to new uses, mainly housing, introducing massive changes in the once rural feel of the place.

World War II

1939–1949

In the 1939–45 global conflict Reading was officially seen as a 'safe place' for administrators as well as thousands of 'at risk' ordinary Londoners or those bombed out from Portsmouth. Thousands of such refugees were billeted in the town, causing the population to swell from 100,000 to 140,000. Anderson shelters and trenches dug in parks for public safety changed the landscape of Reading's gardens and open spaces. New house building stopped in 1940 due to material shortages and in 1941 Reading was declared 'closed' and the Billeting Officer given power to stop the flow of migrants.

There were six air raids by the Luftwaffe between 1940–41 resulting in minor damage and injuries, but the only death was of a milkman's horse in Berkeley Avenue. On 10 February 1943, however, a single Dornier Do217 bomber dropped four bombs that killed 41 people in

the People's Pantry, smashed all the stained glass in St Laurence's Church and blew up the Town Clerk's office. Woodley airfield, supplying ever-increasing numbers of training aircraft for the RAF, and the strategic marshalling yards near Huntley and Palmers' factory, were untouched.

Commandeered Caversham Park House became Spook Central when the BBC moved its 'listening post' activities there to monitor German broadcasts. Speaking 30 languages, many of the translators were refugees from countries over-run by the Axis, and by 1945, were translating a million words a day, including the German surrender note. The landscape legacy of this 'intelligence gathering' is still operational and can be seen in the prominent white satellite dishes arrayed on the grassy slopes on the hillside park.

Intelligence of a more benign kind was stimulated in 1947 when the University of Reading established its main campus at the extensive Whiteknights Estate.

Thrifty Fifties

1950–1959

Rationing was still in place in the whole of the UK until 1954. It was an era of 'mend and do', sensible shoes and steady steadfastness but relieved by the brighter collective thought that things could only get better after war and loss. People did stuff and the political revolution of 1947 led to a plethora of social activism that became established as fact in the 1950s. The NHS, the industrial nationalisation of strategic goods and services and even the creation of National Parks, Areas of Outstanding Natural Beauty and the recording of public rights of way created a shared social, economic and environmental infrastructure. One of the biggest landscape impacts in Reading was the building of massive new estates of council houses. Southcote Estate was commenced in 1950, followed by Emmer Green in Caversham and Whitley Wood (later home to comedian Ricky Gervais) stretched towards the future M4. At the end of the decade new high-rise buildings were erected in Coley and Southcote,

making a massive impact in the landscape and on residents' ability to see more landscapes. In the town centre many of the old traditional family business shops were fading away and new corporate interests taking over; John Lewis acquired Heelas in 1953 although keeping the name. Concrete was replacing the old Reading brick architecture too and causing dissent at the speed of change and transition. Out in the big world the era of the British Empire was crumbling and inward migration from New Elizabethan Commonwealth countries started to patch up the holes in the depleted native workforce. As more former colonies became independent the mix of races arriving in Reading from Africa, India, China and the West Indies created micro-cultures and businesses that still shape the multicultural vitality of the area today.

Sixties and Seventies

1960–1979

With the advent of mass consumption the townscape of Reading changed rapidly to absorb the all-conquering motorcar. In the mid-60s new car production boomed and everyone wanted to be on the roads in their suddenly-affordable PVC-interiored Vauxhall Victors and the like. The Age of the Ford Prefect had arrived and the East-West and North-South routes in and out of Reading, particularly the old coaching route of the A4 London to Bath road, snarled up. To accommodate this surge of metal and rubber the Inner Distribution Road was dreamt up to cater for everyone's transformational transport needs. Sadly the IDR, partly completed in 1969 at the cost of much of Reading's older built core, couldn't cope with the economic boom times of the 1980s and was not finished until 1989. The other solution was to accelerate the building of the southern Reading Bypass. This would take the through traffic and leave local traffic to pootle about un-hindered, as if... This idea was spurred by the construction of a newly fangled motorway from London to Wales following the 'success' of the earlier M1. The concept of the M4 was born in 1956 and by 1961 had managed to bypass Maidenhead. The Maidenhead to Swindon section was not completed until December 1971.

A major intrusion into the landscape with embankments and cuttings, river bridges and new junctions, the M4 was rapidly excavated and constructed, providing a distant boundary to the 'new Reading'. Obviously, there were landowning consortia that saw this as a massive opportunity, and soon the quiet landscape of farm fields and lanes leading down to the marshes and watermills of the river Loddon became from 1977 'Lower Earley', the site of 'Europe's Biggest Housing Estate'. Naturally this attracted 30,000 more inward migrants who now had a new motorway to play with and several new junctions to speed their journeys away from Reading. Those that did find work inside Reading now clogged up the older arterial road system with thousands of new cars. The rapid spread of look-alike private estates with cul-de-sac lifestyles gobbled up every available space as land uses changed from local produce supply to breezeblock and concrete pantile paradises. Supermarkets arose and spread in the town centre and then spread some more.

Britain (and Reading) were rejoined to Europe in 1975 after an overwhelming 67% majority vote in favour at an EEC referendum.

Eighties and Nineties

1980–1999

The era of computers and the fledgling internet made big changes to people's *outlook* on mobility and working practices but the geographical inertia of office-based work was a tough one to crack and change was slow. Offices continued to be built and Reading gathered more

focus as an alternative employment centre to London, with the development of Green Park close to the M4 as a key new centre for multi-national companies and those wanting quick access to the motorway network. IT became a big high-tech industrial employer with companies such as Digital leading a Hydrated Silicon Valley revolution in the watery Thames Valley.

The Green Park development was enormous in its ambition and scope and covered a seemingly undeveloped segment in the southwest corner of the map of Reading. However, as soon as the archaeological investigations began as part of the planning mitigation measures, it revealed an amazing succession of Neolithic, Bronze Age, Iron Age and Roman age 'settlements' dubbed the 'biggest prehistoric housing estate in Europe'.

Energy was also high on the landscape-altering agenda with the closure of the 'relief' power station at Earley made redundant as a result of the opening of the mega coal-powered power station at Didcot. Here, the cooling towers and chimneys were labelled 'the cathedral of the vale' with horsetail plumes of exhaust gases forming new cloudscapes visible for fifty miles in all directions. Vast amounts of energy produced by the coalmines and resultant messy landscapes of Nottinghamshire (and latterly Russia, Colombia and Australia via Avonmouth docks) fuelled not only the growth of Swindon and Reading but also atomic Harwell and the Joint European Torus nuclear fusion lab. Earley power station was quickly removed from the landscape to make way for a new high-tech IT industrial park and half a start on a motorway bridge across the Thames Valley.

With the free movement of peoples granted within the EU more inward migration occurred from European countries, with opportunities in construction, maintenance, hospitality, the NHS and agriculture readily available.

The New Millennium

2000–2015

The dreaded 'millennium bug' failed to ravage the expanding IT land-scape of Reading's new digital industrial base and fireworks ushered in the next 1000 years. Henry Marchant, a civil servant of Reading, would have joined the nation's stand-by army of St Georges to fight this digital dragon but instead retired to bed.

In the 2000s, major landscape and townscape changes were planned and slowly implemented. Some of these have far-reaching impacts. In the vertical plane Green Park's 2 MW wind turbine and the spiky new office block, the Blade, strutted skywards. The adjacent Reading Gaol, famous throughout the literary world because of one imprisoned poet, designed by George Gilbert Scott but based on the style of Philadelphia Penitentiary, Pennsylvania, was decreed to be surplus to requirements by HMP and its future as a Victorian brick icon is under scrutiny. The Oracle, the amoeba-like temple of Christmas shopping frenzy, calls to its customers from the site of Kendrick's Kennet-side workhouse.

The last flight of Concorde took place on 24 October 2003. The supersonic plane's flight path invariably intruded into Reading's 'airscape' albeit in subsonic mode and for two decades demonstrably rattled the town's windowpanes several times a day. Bigger, more frequent, but marginally less noisy planes now float through the air using the Woodley NDB (non-directional beacon) as a marker.

The most widespread visible change is the future face of the railway system. The much-delayed rebuilding of Reading Station and the awesome concrete railway flyover finally proceeded in concert

with the announcement that the Paddington to Bristol and Wales mainline would be electrified. This is one of the most intrusive landscape impacts on Reading since Isambard Kingdom Brunel's original railway. Tens of thousands of line-side trees and shrubs have been eradicated, some of which, in the great Sonning cutting, were probably as old as the GWR itself. These aged trees, these graceful air fresheners, are being replaced by the sticks of steel and metal gantries that will carry the overhead electric wires for the Japanese-designed and built electric bullet-ish trains.

Reading Year of Culture 2016

2016 saw a year of artistic celebration and stimulation in Reading. It had deep resonance with the past, the heritage of place and peoples that this book extols and Reading's six wonderful museums (including the Museum of English Rural Life and Museum of Reading) tell intriguing stories of past lives and events. These amazing collections are continuously updating the jigsaw of the past and adding the culture of the moment to their stocks. It was also the year that Britain, or some parts of it, but not Reading, voted to leave the EU by the narrow margin of 52% to 48%, albeit that nobody knows what this could mean for Reading's people, landscape and economy in the future. Four days after that the tiny country of Iceland with a population comparable to greater Reading humbled the England football team in an act of poetic justice on a piece of green grass in Nice.

The relationship between function and morphology in landscape is important to memory. Many thousands of people come to Reading and associate the place with the annual Reading Festival, for others it was 16 years of WOMAD or events hosted by the Madejski Stadium, the Hexagon, Beer Festival, Pride, the Progress Theatre, Reading Concert Hall or South Street Arts Centre. Reading Rock Festival can only occur because the flat, floodplain landscape provides enough space for the camping needs of 87,000 temporary residents. On the local stage, in countless buildings or in the open air, the unassuming talents of here-and-now people, musicians, dancers, singers, actors, painters, sculptors, writers and poets are offered. The Whiteknights Studio Trail lifts the carpet to discover a spangled felty underlay of brilliant artists working hard just beneath the surface of international stardom but equally as good.

Two Rivers Press, and its outstanding Mr Real Reading himself, the late Pete Hay, has had significant influence within the mental map of the borders of the town. The seminal book of place *Where Two Rivers Meet* written with Adam Stout is probably one of the best exposures of the realities of the cultural importance of tiny things in the lives of real people that has ever been created. It is here, in these gritty damp alluvial soils of everyday experience, that the roots of the intellectual plants that create the rich flowering of artistic and cultural feelings are propagated. These soils, of the places we live in and call 'home', are important because we also imbue them with richness through our participation. There is a book in everyone and an artist in us all but it is the form of place and functional experiences of place that interact to create beauty. This beauty requires freedom and nourishment to make every year a year of culture.

Future Landscapes of the City of Reading

Will there be opportunity to bring to life the creative potential for Reading by letting the people of the city re-imagine the landscape that future generations might want to live in? It is clearly a place that seems to develop independent thinking, as William Cobbett said in *Rural Rides* in 1822, 'I am delighted with the people that I have seen at Reading'. The film *The Matrix* explored the thesis that perhaps the 'reality' we experience in our minds is not the only reality, and will Redingistas, some time hence, simply digitally enhance their brains' sense of place to suit their personal preferences? Might it be possible to conjure a beautiful brick walled beer garden in the Gothic style of Waterhouse planted with exotic seeds and perambulated by fascinated folk nibbling exquisite biscuits?

Many things come together in designing a city of the future but Reading is not a blank canvas. Most developing city centres nest like cuckoo chicks in existing settlements and attempt to take them over by building enormously high Central Business Districts by way of defining a phallic presence of masculine domination. Reading is the home to the oldest known polyphonic secular English song 'Sumer is Icumen In. Lhu-de sing cuc-cu' but what if it abandoned the cuckoo nest model and became a place of beauty, peacefulness and green-ery instead? Reading is constrained by the topographical physicality of its river valleys and the hostile tribes on the northern bank of the Thames. If traffic congestion is currently a major economic problem it might only get worse as the future population increases. Traffic is grossly noisy, an occupier of public space (the road network) and is a lethal polluting health hazard. Some cities, such as Hamburg, Freiburg, Madrid and Copenhagen, are moving towards car-free city status. Hamburg intends to be car-free by 2030 and is promoting inter-

linked green spaces covering 40% of the city so that pedestrians and cyclists can make the majority of their journeys actively, healthily and safely. Copenhagen already has a large number of residents who have opted to give up a private car because the alternatives are so much cheaper and healthier. Could Reading follow this enlightened trend and outshine London? London is considering becoming a National Park City and Birmingham wants to join an international group of Biophyllic Cities so should Reading aim for city status as the first Area of Outstanding Urban Beauty?

Everyone has the chance to create the landscape Reading could become by joining in with Futurescape 2050: Be creative, paint the town red, celebrate the place of the people of the Red One.

Further information

Abattoirs to Zin-Zan; Sowan, A; Two Rivers Press, 2000

A Community Right to Beauty; Harvey, A and Julian, C; ResPublica, 2015

A Much Maligned Town Opinions of Reading 1586–1997; Sowan, A, Hay, P and Hall, P; Two Rivers Press, 1997

At the Sign of the Hop Leaf; www.simondsfamily.me.uk

Bizarre Berkshire; Mackay, D; Two Rivers Press, 2012

Broad Street Chapel & the Origins of Dissent in Reading; Sawers, G; Two Rivers Press, 2012

Bronze Age Britain; Parker Pearson, M; Batsford Ltd/English Heritage; 1993

England in Particular; Clifford, S and King, A; Hodder and Stoughton, 2006

European Landscape Convention; Council of Europe; Strasbourg, France; www.coe.int/en/web/landscape/home

Evidence for an extra-terrestrial impact 12,900 years ago that contributed to the mega-faunal extinctions and the Younger Dryas cooling; Firestone, R, West, A, Kennett, J; Proceedings of the National Academy of Science, Vol. 104, No. 41, 9 October 2007

Flora Britannica; Mabey, R; Sinclair Stevenson, 1996

Greater London National Park City Draft Charter; Raven-Ellison, D; 2015 (NationalParkCity.London@LondonNPC)

Royal County of Berkshire History; Ford, D; www.berkshirehistory.com

Homo Britannicus; Stringer, C; Allen Lane; 2006

Jude the Obscure; Hardy, T; Penguin Classics, 2003

Lexicon of named rock units; British Geological Survey; www.bgs.ac.uk

Museum of English Rural Life; www.reading.ac.uk/merl

Reading Museum: Town Hall; www.readingmuseum.org.uk

Reading Museum: Riverside at Blake's Lock;
   www.readingmuseum.org.uk

Reading Past and Present; Hylton, S; Sutton Publishing, 2000

Reading UK 2050; www.livingreading.co.uk

Rural Rides; Cobbett, W; Penguin, 1981

Silchester Iron Age finds reveal secrets of pre-Roman Britain;
   Kennedy, M; *The Guardian* 31 July 2012

The Avebury Cycle; Dames, M; Thames & Hudson, 1996

*The Celebrated Reading Sauce: Charles Cocks and Co Ltd
   1789–1962*; Corley, T; Berkshire Archaeology Journal Vol. 70
   (Archaeological Data Service)

*The Culture of Cloth in Early Modern England: Textual Construction
   of National Identity*; Hentschell, R; Routledge, 2008

The History of Suttons; www.suttons.co.uk

The Huntley and Palmers Collection: Reading Biscuit Town;
   www.huntleyandpalmers.org.uk

The Making of the English Landscape; Hoskins, WG; Penguin, 1988

*The Penguin Atlas of World History (from the Beginning to the Eve
   of the French Revolution)*; Hilgemann, W and Kinder, H;
   Penguin Books Ltd., 1974

The Secret Thames; Mackay, D; Ebury Press 1992

The Story of Reading; Phillips, D; Countryside Books, 1980

*The Upper Palaeolithic and Mesolithic of Berkshire: The Thames
   and Solent Research Framework*; Barnett, C; 2009

The Village Labourer, 1760–1832, Hammond, B and Hammond, J;
   Longmans, Green & Co, 1912

Where Two Rivers Meet; Hay, P and Stout, A; Two Rivers Press, 1994

Two Rivers Press has been publishing in and about Reading since 1994. Founded by the artist Peter Hay (1951–2003), the press continues to delight readers, local and further afield, with its varied list of individually designed, thought-provoking books.